A CHILD'S CHRISTMAS IN WALES

A Child's Christmas in Wales

A STORY BY DYLAN THOMAS
with woodcuts by Ellen Raskin

J. M. Dent   London

A CHILD'S CHRISTMAS IN WALES

One Christmas was so much like another,
in those years around the sea-town corner now
and out of all sound except the distant speaking
of the voices I sometimes hear a moment before sleep,
that I can never remember whether it snowed
for six days and six nights when I was twelve
or whether it snowed for twelve days and
twelve nights when I was six.

All the Christmases roll down toward the
two-tongued sea, like a cold and headlong moon
bundling down the sky that was our street;
and they stop at the rim of the ice-edged,
fish-freezing waves, and I plunge my hands in the
snow and bring out whatever I can find. In goes
my hand into that wool-white bell-tongued ball of
holidays resting at the rim of the carol-singing
sea, and out come Mrs Prothero and the firemen.

It was on the afternoon of the day
of Christmas Eve, and I was in Mrs Prothero's
garden, waiting for cats, with her son Jim.
It was snowing. It was always snowing at Christmas.
December, in my memory, is white as Lapland,
though there were no reindeers.
But there were cats. Patient, cold and callous,
our hands wrapped in socks, we waited
to snowball the cats. Sleek and long as jaguars
and horrible-whiskered, spitting and snarling,

they would slink and sidle over the white
back-garden walls, and the lynx-eyed hunters,
Jim and I, fur-capped and moccasined trappers
from Hudson Bay, off Mumbles Road, would hurl
our deadly snowballs at the green of their eyes.

The wise cats never appeared. We were so still,
Eskimo-footed arctic marksmen in the muffling
silence of the eternal snows—eternal,
ever since Wednesday—that we never heard
Mrs Prothero's first cry from her igloo at the
bottom of the garden. Or, if we heard it at all,

it was, to us, like the far-off challenge of our enemy
and prey, the neighbour's polar cat. But soon the
voice grew louder. 'Fire!' cried Mrs Prothero,
and she beat the dinner-gong.

And we ran down the garden, with the snowballs
in our arms, toward the house; and smoke,
indeed, was pouring out of the dining-room,
and the gong was bombilating, and Mrs Prothero
was announcing ruin like a town crier in Pompeii.
This was better than all the cats in Wales
standing on the wall in a row. We bounded into
the house, laden with snowballs, and stopped at
the open door of the smoke-filled room.

Something was burning all right;
perhaps it was Mr Prothero, who always slept
there after midday dinner with a newspaper
over his face. But he was standing in the middle
of the room, saying, 'A fine Christmas!'

and smacking at the smoke with a slipper.
'Call the fire brigade,' cried Mrs Prothero
as she beat the gong.

'They won't be there,' said Mr Prothero,
'it's Christmas.'

There was no fire to be seen, only clouds of smoke
and Mr Prothero standing in the middle of them,
waving his slipper as though he were conducting.

'Do something,' he said.

And we threw all our snowballs into the smoke—
I think we missed Mr Prothero—and ran out

of the house to the telephone box.

'Let's call the police as well,' Jim said.

'And the ambulance.'

'And Ernie Jenkins, he likes fires.'

But we only called the fire brigade, and soon
the fire engine came and three tall men in helmets
brought a hose into the house and Mr Prothero
got out just in time before they turned it on.
Nobody could have had a noisier Christmas Eve.
And when the firemen turned off the hose and
were standing in the wet, smoky room, Jim's aunt,
Miss Prothero, came downstairs and peered in
at them. Jim and I waited, very quietly, to hear what
she would say to them. She said the right thing,
always. She looked at the three tall firemen in their
shining helmets, standing among the smoke and
cinders and dissolving snowballs, and she said:
'Would you like anything to read?'

Years and years and years ago, when I was a boy,
when there were wolves in Wales, and birds
the colour of red-flannel petticoats whisked past
the harp-shaped hills, when we sang and wallowed
all night and day in caves that smelt like Sunday
afternoons in damp front farmhouse parlours,
and we chased, with the jawbones of deacons,
the English and the bears, before the motor-car,
before the wheel, before the duchess-faced horse,
when we rode the daft and happy hills bareback,
it snowed and it snowed. But here a small boy says:
'It snowed last year, too. I made a snowman and

my brother knocked it down and I knocked my
brother down and then we had tea.'

'But that was not the same snow,' I say.
'Our snow was not only shaken from whitewash
buckets down the sky, it came shawling out of the ground
and swam and drifted out of the arms and hands and
bodies of the trees; snow grew overnight on the
roofs of the houses like a pure and grandfather
moss, minutely white-ivied the walls and settled on
the postman, opening the gate, like a dumb, numb
thunderstorm of white, torn Christmas cards.'

'Were there postmen then, too?'
'With sprinkling eyes and wind-cherried noses,
on spread, frozen feet they crunched up to the
doors and mittened on them manfully. But all that
the children could hear was a ringing of bells.'

'You mean that the postman went rat-a-tat-tat
and the doors rang?'

'I mean that the bells that the children could hear were inside them.'

'I only hear thunder sometimes, never bells.'

'There were church bells, too.'

'Inside them?'

'No, no, no, in the bat-black, snow-white belfries, tugged by bishops and storks. And they rang their tidings over the bandaged town, over the frozen foam of the powder and ice-cream hills, over the crackling sea. It seemed that all the

churches boomed for joy under my window; and
the weathercocks crew for Christmas, on our fence.'

'Get back to the postmen.'

'They were just ordinary postmen, fond of walking
and dogs and Christmas and the snow.
They knocked on the doors with blue knuckles. . . .'

'Ours has got a black knocker. . . .'

'And then they stood on the white Welcome mat in
the little, drifted porches and huffed and puffed,
making ghosts with their breath, and jogged from
foot to foot like small boys wanting to go out.'

'And then the Presents?'

'And then the Presents, after the Christmas box.
And the cold postman, with a rose on his
button-nose, tingled down the tea-tray-slithered run
of the chilly glinting hill. He went in his ice-bound
boots like a man on fishmonger's slabs. He wagged his

bag like a frozen camel's hump, dizzily turned the corner on one foot, and, by God, he was gone.'

'Get back to the Presents.'

'There were the Useful Presents: engulfing mufflers of the old coach days, and mittens made for giant sloths; zebra scarfs of a substance like silky gum that could be tug-o'-warred down to the galoshes; blinding tam-o'-shanters like patchwork tea cosies and bunny-suited busbies and balaclavas for victims of head-shrinking tribes; from aunts who always

wore wool next to the skin there were moustached and
rasping vests that made you wonder why the aunts
had any skin left at all; and once I had a little
crocheted nose bag from an aunt now, alas,
no longer whinnying with us. And pictureless books
in which small boys, though warned with quotations
not to, *would* skate on Farmer Giles' pond
and did and drowned; and books that told me
everything about the wasp, except why.'

'Go on to the Useless Presents.'

'Bags of moist and many-coloured jelly babies
and a folded flag and a false nose and a tram-
conductor's cap and a machine that punched tickets
and rang a bell; never a catapult; once, by mistake
that no one could explain, a little hatchet;
and a celluloid duck that made, when you pressed it,
a most unducklike sound, a mewing moo that an
ambitious cat might make who wished to be a cow;
and a painting book in which I could make the grass,

the trees, the sea and the animals any colour
I pleased, and still the dazzling sky-blue sheep
are grazing in the red field under the
rainbow-billed and pea-green birds.

Hardboileds, toffee, fudge and allsorts, crunches,
cracknels, humbugs, glaciers, marzipan, and
butterwelsh for the Welsh. And troops of
bright tin soldiers who, if they could not fight,
could always run. And Snakes-and-Families
and Happy Ladders. And Easy Hobbi-Games
for Little Engineers, complete with instructions.

Oh, easy for Leonardo! And a whistle to make
the dogs bark to wake up the old man next door
to make him beat on the wall with his stick
to shake our picture off the wall.
And a packet of cigarettes: you put one
in your mouth and you stood at the corner
of the street and you waited for hours, in vain,
for an old lady to scold you for smoking
a cigarette, and then with a smirk you ate it.
And then it was breakfast under the balloons.'

'Were there Uncles like in our house?'

'There are always Uncles at Christmas.
The same Uncles. And on Christmas mornings,
with dog-disturbing whistle and sugar fags,
I would scour the swatched town for the news of
the little world, and find always a dead bird
by the white Post Office or by the deserted swings;
perhaps a robin, all but one of his fires out.
Men and women wading or scooping back from chapel,

with taproom noses and wind-bussed cheeks,
all albinos, huddled their stiff black jarring
feathers against the irreligious snow.

Mistletoe hung from the gas brackets in all
the front parlours; there was sherry and walnuts
and bottled beer and crackers by the dessertspoons;
and cats in their fur-abouts watched the fires;
and the high-heaped fire spat, all ready for
the chestnuts and the mulling pokers.

Some few large men sat in the front parlours,
without their collars, Uncles almost certainly,
trying their new cigars, holding them out
judiciously at arms' length, returning them
to their mouths, coughing, then holding them out
again as though waiting for the explosion;
and some few small Aunts, not wanted in the kitchen,
nor anywhere else for that matter, sat on the
very edges of their chairs, poised and brittle,
afraid to break, like faded cups and saucers.'

Not many those mornings trod the piling streets:
an old man always, fawn-bowlered, yellow-gloved
and, at this time of year, with spats of snow,
would take his constitutional to the white bowling
green and back, as he would take it wet or fine
on Christmas Day or Doomsday; sometimes two hale
young men, with big pipes blazing, no overcoats
and wind-blown scarfs, would trudge, unspeaking,
down to the forlorn sea, to work up an appetite,

to blow away the fumes, who knows, to walk
into the waves until nothing of them was left
but the two curling smoke clouds of their
inextinguishable briars. Then I would be
slap-dashing home, the gravy smell of the dinners
of others, the bird smell, the brandy, the
pudding and mince, coiling up to my nostrils, when
out of a snow-clogged side lane would come a boy
the spit of myself, with a pink-tipped cigarette
and the violet past of a black eye, cocky
as a bullfinch, leering all to himself.

I hated him on sight and sound, and would be
about to put my dog whistle to my lips
and blow him off the face of Christmas when
suddenly he, with a violet wink, put *his* whistle
to *his* lips and blew so stridently, so high,
so exquisitely loud, that gobbling faces,
their cheeks bulged with goose, would press
against their tinselled windows, the whole length
of the white echoing street. For dinner
we had turkey and blazing pudding, and after
dinner the Uncles sat in front of the fire,
loosened all buttons, put their large moist
hands over their watch chains, groaned a little
and slept. Mothers, aunts and sisters scuttled
to and fro, bearing tureens. Auntie Bessie, who
had already been frightened, twice, by a
clock-work mouse, whimpered at the sideboard
and had some elderberry wine. The dog was sick.
Auntie Dosie had to have three aspirins,
but Auntie Hannah, who liked port, stood in

the middle of the snowbound back yard, singing
like a big-bosomed thrush. I would blow up
ballons to see how big they would blow up to;
and, when they burst, which they all did,
the Uncles jumped and rumbled. In the rich
and heavy afternoon, the Uncles breathing
like dolphins and the snow descending,
I would sit among festoons and Chinese lanterns
and nibble dates and try to make a model man-o' war,
following the Instructions for Little Engineers,
and produce what might be mistaken for
a sea-going tramcar.

Or I would go out, my bright new boots
squeaking, into the white world, on to the
seaward hill, to call on Jim and Dan and Jack
and to pad through the still streets, leaving
huge deep footprints on the hidden pavements.

'I bet people will think there's been hippos.'

'What would you do if you saw a hippo
coming down our street?'

'I'd go like this, bang! I'd throw him over
the railings and roll him down the hill and then
I'd tickle him under the ear and he'd wag his tail.'

'What would you do if you saw *two* hippos?'

Iron-flanked and bellowing he-hippos clanked
and battered through the scudding snow toward us
as we passed Mr Daniel's house.

'Let's post Mr Daniel a snowball through
his letter-box.'

'Let's write things in the snow.'

'Let's write, "Mr Daniel looks like a spaniel"
all over his lawn.'

Or we walked on the white shore.
'Can the fishes see it's snowing?'

The silent one-clouded heavens drifted on to the sea.
Now we were snow-blind travellers lost on the
north hills, and vast dewlapped dogs, with flasks
round their necks, ambled and shambled up to us,

baying "Excelsior". We returned home through the
poor streets where only a few children fumbled
with bare red fingers in the wheel-rutted snow
and cat-called after us, their voices fading away,
as we trudged uphill, into the cries of the dock
birds and the hooting of ships out in the whirling
bay. And then, at tea the recovered Uncles would
be jolly; and the ice cake loomed in the centre of
the table like a marble grave. Auntie Hannah laced
her tea with rum, because it was only once a year.

Bring out the tall tales now that we told
by the fire as the gaslight bubbled like a diver.
Ghosts whooed like owls in the long nights
when I dared not look over my shoulder; animals
lurked in the cubbyhole under the stairs where the
gas meter ticked. And I remember that we went
singing carols once, when there wasn't the shaving
of a moon to light the flying streets. At the end
of a long road was a drive that led to a large

house, and we stumbled up the darkness of the drive
that night, each one of us afraid, each one holding
a stone in his hand in case, and all of us too brave
to say a word. The wind through the trees
made noises as of old and unpleasant and maybe
webfooted men wheezing in caves. We reached
the black bulk of the house.

'What shall we give them? Hark the Herald?'

'No,' Jack said, 'Good King Wenceslas.
I'll count three.'

One, two, three, and we began to sing,
our voices high and seemingly distant in the
snow-felted darkness round the house that
was occupied by nobody we knew. We stood
close together, near the dark door.

Good King Wenceslas looked out
On the Feast of Stephen . . .

And then a small, dry voice, like the voice
of someone who has not spoken for a long time,
joined our singing: a small, dry, eggshell voice
from the other side of the door: a small dry voice
through the keyhole. And when we stopped running
we were outside *our* house; the front room was lovely;
balloons floated under the hot-water-bottle-gulping gas;
everything was good again and shone over the town.

'Perhaps it was a ghost,' Jim said.

'Perhaps it was trolls,' Dan said,
who was always reading.

'Let's go in and see if there's any jelly left,'
Jack said. And we did that.

Always on Christmas night there was music.
An uncle played the fiddle, a cousin sang
'Cherry Ripe', and another uncle sang 'Drake's Drum'.
It was very warm in the little house.
Auntie Hannah, who had got on to the parsnip
wine, sang a song about Bleeding Hearts and Death,
and then another in which she said her heart
was like a Bird's Nest; and then everybody

laughed again; and then I went to bed.
Looking through my bedroom window, out into
the moonlight and the unending smoke-coloured snow,
I could see the lights in the windows
of all the other houses on our hill and hear
the music rising from them up the long, steadily
falling night. I turned the gas down, I got
into bed. I said some words to the close and
holy darkness, and then I slept.